THE PORTABLE CRAFTER
RIBBONWORK

THE PORTABLE CRAFTER
RIBBONWORK

Katheryn Tidwell Bieber

Sterling Publishing Co., Inc.
New York
A Sterling/Chapelle Book

Chapelle, Ltd., Inc.,
P.O. Box 9252, Ogden, UT 84409
(801) 621-2777 • (801) 621-2788 Fax
e-mail: chapelle@chapelleltd.com
Web site: chapelleltd.com

Library of Congress Cataloging-in-Publication Data

Bieber, Katheryn Tidwell.
    The portable crafter. Ribbonwork / Katheryn Tidwell Bieber.
        p. cm.
    "A Sterling/Chapelle Book."
    Includes index.
    ISBN 1-4027-2141-2
1. Ribbon work. I. Tite: Ribbonwork. II. Title.

TT850.5.B54 2005
746'.0476--dc22   2005001196

Published by Sterling Publishing Co., Inc.
387 Park Avenue South, New York, NY 10016
©2005 by Katheryn Tidwell Bieber
Distributed in Canada by Sterling Publishing
c/o Canadian Manda Group, One Atlantic Avenue, Suite 105
Toronto, Ontario, Canada M6K 3E7
Distributed in Great Britain by Chrysalis Books Group PLC,
The Chrysalis Building, Bramley Road, London W10 6SP, England
Distributed in Australia by Capricorn Link (Australia) Pty. Ltd.
P.O. Box 704, Windsor, NSW 2756, Australia
Printed in China
All Rights Reserved

Sterling ISBN 1-4027-2141-2

For information about custom editions, special sales, premium
and corporate purchases, please contact Sterling Special Sales
Department at 800-805-5489 or specialsales@sterlingpub.com.

TABLE OF CONTENTS

A bit of fragrance always clings to the hand that gives the rose. This phrase reminds me that when I create a gift for another person, a smile will come to their face every time they see it, remembering the love with which it was made. This book is filled with projects that make great gifts, as well as things for you to enjoy. The best part is that they are all easy and fun to make.

As a busy mom with five wonderful children, I have learned the value of how much can be done in a fifteen-minute time block. Time and energy can elude me as I run around attempting to accomplish all that needs to be done, but I fill my life with meaningful and creative moments that build upon each other. You can do this, too.

I love the feeling that creating things gives to me, and I love sharing my creativity with others.

Many of these projects or pieces of these projects were done while waiting to pick up children at school or activities. I want to share with you how "by doing small and simple things," great things can be accomplished, fifteen minutes at a time.

RIBBONWORK BASICS

The projects in *The Portable Crafter: Ribbonwork* were selected so that you can work on them while you are on the go, waiting at the doctor's office, or in the carpool line. However, with any project there are some ribbonwork basics that should be considered before you step out of the door.

SUPPLIES
Resealable Plastic Bags

To keep ribbonwork items such as leaves and flowers clean and organized, use resealable plastic bags. Before starting a project, separate the flowers, leaves, and supplies, each into their own bag. You can even buy a bag designed for vegetables that has very small holes in it. This keeps the bags from holding excess air, yet still keeps the supplies clean. Toss the bags in a favorite "tote" or project basket.

Threads

The two types of thread used for the projects in this book are hand-quilting thread and beading floss. Hand-quilting thread is used to make the hand-gathering stitches and to hold or stitch items together. Beading floss is used for making tiny "invisible" stitches, tacking down loose loopy petals and ribbon embroidery stitches, and adding beads and crystals.

When making hand-gathering stitches for most of these projects, use long stitches ⅛". If making tiny quilting stitches, it becomes very difficult to pull up the gathers, especially when using velvet ribbons.

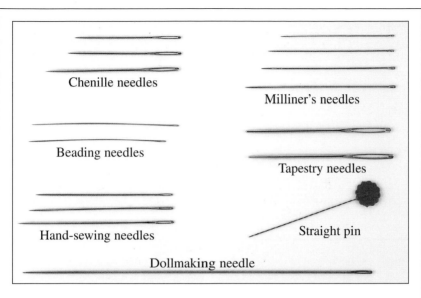

Chenille needles

Milliner's needles

Beading needles

Tapestry needles

Hand-sewing needles

Straight pin

Dollmaking needle

Needles

Use a chenille needle for ribbon embroidery. This is a long needle with a large eye and a point that is not too sharp. Most of the designs in this book use sizes 16–22.

A milliner's needle is a favorite for making roses and leaves. It is quite long, thin, and easy to hold in your hands.

Beading needles are very fine, long needles with a long narrow eye.

Other Sewing Supplies

• Craft scissors
• Fabric scissors
• Straight pins

TYPES OF RIBBON

Cross-dyed Ribbon

Cross-dyed ribbon is woven with two different thread colors (one in each direction), so the ribbon seems to change colors in the light as it is moved.

Ombre ribbon

Variegated ribbon

Double-faced satin ribbon

Velvet ribbon

Cross-dyed organdy ribbon

Organdy ribbon

Netting ribbon

Dyed knitting ribbon

Hand-dyed silk ribbon

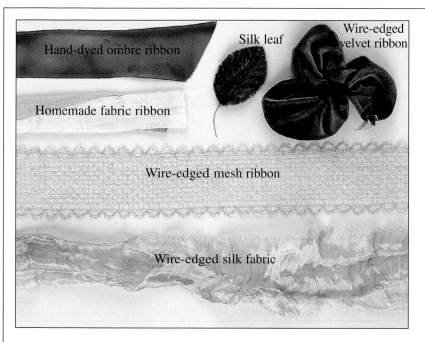

Hand-dyed ombre ribbon

Silk leaf

Wire-edged velvet ribbon

Homemade fabric ribbon

Wire-edged mesh ribbon

Wire-edged silk fabric

Variegated and Ombre Ribbons

These ribbons change in color across the length or width of the ribbon. The ribbon is referred to as ombre if it changes color in the same color family, for example from pink to fuchsia. The ribbon is variegated if it changes color in a different color family, for example from purple to green.

Organdy Ribbon

This is a sheer, chiffon-type ribbon.

Hand-dyed Silk Ribbon

This silk ribbon has a variation in color because it has been dyed by hand.

Wire Ribbons

Working with wire-edged ribbon is fun. It has fine wires woven into its edges. Remember not to use fabric scissors when cutting wire-mesh or wired-edged ribbon, because it will dull the blades. Use an old or inexpensive pair of craft scissors or wire cutters to cut wire ribbons.

Wire-mesh ribbon or fabric is woven entirely from wire in one direction and colored threads in the other. It tends to be rather sheer and very elegant to work with when making projects.

Satin Ribbon

Double-faced satin ribbon is a tightly woven ribbon that has been around forever. In this book, we will give it a new look by adding some fabric dyes.

Ribbon Width as a Measurement

"Ribbon width" is the width of the ribbon. If I give the ribbon widths for a project, the "formula" will work for any width of ribbon.

Making Ribbons

While this book is in the *Portable Crafter* series, it is best to spend a little time in preparation at the sewing machine. By making your own ribbons, you can really customize your flowers to match or accent any home, clothing, or wedding colors perfectly. Even using silk fabrics, it is relatively inexpensive.

1. Cut (or tear along the grain line) fabrics into 2" strips. Lay one strip from each of the two different fabrics with right sides together, and sew ¼" seam allowance along each edge.

2. Stitch across one short edge; then pinning a safety pin to this edge, turn the fabric right side out and press the edges.

3. Cut "ribbon" into appropriate lengths for the projects.

BASES/BACKING

Crinoline and Buckram

Crinoline and buckram look like starched cheesecloth. Crinoline is a lighter weight than buckram. Crinoline and buckram can be used as a base for a flower. See Sweetheart Rose on page 21.

Cardboard

Cardboard makes a nice backing to glue or stitch to the back of any ribbon flower. Simply adjust the size of the circle or oval of fabric and cardboard to fit the project.

1. Run a hand-gathering stitch around the fabric circle or oval and pull up the gathers slightly.

2. Place over cardboard circle or oval and pull up gathers tightly, knotting to secure.

Silk Leaves

Another way to finish the back of a flower is to glue silk leaves onto the back. The leaves add a little support and look nice.

EMBELLISHMENTS

Vintage Jewelry

Use vintage jewelry in ribbon-work designs. If it is a very special piece of vintage jewelry or a family heirloom, hand-tack onto the project with strong quilting thread at pin-backed fastener on the back of the vintage jewelry. This way it will not be lost if it becomes unpinned, and the vintage jewelry can be removed and worn on something else. If the vintage jewelry is of no significant value, adhere jewelry with industrial-strength glue.

Crystal Beads

Accent roses with crystal beads or vintage rhinestones. It creates a dewdrop look on a rose petal.

STITCHES TO KNOW

French Knot

1. Bring needle up through fabric and wrap ribbon loosely two or three times around needle close to sharp point.

2. Hold ribbon off to one side as you gently insert needle next to entry hole.

3. Hold this knot until ribbon is pulled all the way through to back of fabric.

Leaf Stitch

1. Bring ribbon up through the fabric. Lay ribbon flat against fabric.

2. Pierce ribbon near one edge of ribbon on your way back down through fabric to create a soft "leaf" at end of this stitch.

3. Pull ribbon through gently so that you do not lose this soft "leaf."

Ribbon Stitch

1. Bring ribbon up through fabric. Lay ribbon flat against fabric.

2. Pierce center of ribbon on your way back down through fabric to create a soft curl at end of this stitch. Pull ribbon through gently so that you do not lose this soft curl.

Running Stitch

1. Bring needle up through the fabric. Insert needle down through fabric, creating a straight stitch. Repeat, leaving an unstitched area between each stitch.

Whipped Running Stitch

1. Complete a running stitch.

2. Go under first running stitch. Be careful not to pierce fabric or catch the running stitch. Come up on the other side of the stitch. Keeping the thread flat, wrap over the stitch and go under the next running stitch. Continue in this same manner.

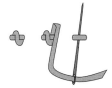

RIBBON EMBROIDERY GUIDELINES

Threading and Locking Ribbon onto Needle

To cut down on the amount of wear and tear while embroidering with silk ribbons, work with 14"–18" lengths of ribbon at a time.

1. Cut end of ribbon at a diagonal and thread it through a needle with a large eye, depending on the width and texture of the ribbon.

2. "Lock" ribbon onto needle pushing needle through center of the ribbon approximately ½" from one end. Pull on opposite end of the ribbon to lock ribbon onto eye of needle.

Keeping It Loose! Loosen Up!

When embroidering with ribbon, make loose and relaxed stitches rather than tight stitches, as when using floss or doing traditional embroidery. These ribbons want to fluff, curl, and roll, adding a wonderful dimension to the designs. If you pull the ribbons too tightly while stitching, you will lose the dimension that creates these lovely designs.

Finishing the Back of Ribbon Embroidery

Finish the back of ribbon embroidery by using the following steps to knot the ribbons:

1. Bring ribbon to back of fabric. Trim end of ribbon to ¾".

2. Hand-stitch to back side of fabric with needle and thread.

TECHNIQUES

Cabbage Rose

1. Make a folded and rolled rose. See Folded and Rolled Rose on page 18.

2. Thread size 13 chenille needle with 15" of 1½"-wide silk ribbon. Stitch seven base petals for each large rose. Refer to Ribbon Stitch on page 14. Use the ribbon-stitch to tack folded and rolled rose, slightly off-center, near middle of base petals.

3. Stitch long and loose petals between base petals and folded and rolled rose. To do this: Bring needle up through base petals, then bring it down again ⅓" from where you brought it up. Let ribbon fall in a soft loop. Repeat around sides and bottom of rose.

4. Hand-tack petals with matching color thread.

Fabric Bridal Rose

1. Make rose center from a 7" length of 1½"-wide ribbon, See Folded and Rolled Rose on page 18.

2. Cut nine 5" lengths from ribbon for leaves.

3. Fold each end of ribbon down toward back. Hand-gather-stitch in a straight line across bottom of ribbon, catching ends you have folded down in the gathering stitch.

4. Pull up gathers tightly; knot to secure.

5. Stitch each petal individually around center of rose.

Folded Leaves and Buds

1. Fold one end of 5" ribbon length over the other, forming a cone shape. Run a gathering stitch from right to left at bottom edge of where the ribbon overlaps. Pull running-stitch into a gather. Wrap thread around twice; knot to secure.

2. To make a bud: Follow Step 1 above in desired ribbon color for bud.

Folded and Rolled Rose

1. Fold one end of ribbon diagonally 1½" from end.

2. Fold diagonal end in half. Tack in place with a couple of stitches. Fold excess ribbon back diagonally, then roll base tightly down and

around corner and onto ribbon edge. Tack again at base.

3. Fold ribbon back and repeat rolling and tacking process to add new petals.

4. Make larger outermost petals by increasing length of diagonal fold. To finish rose: Hand-gather-stitch last few inches of ribbon and curve stitches up to top edge of ribbon as you get to the end.

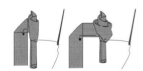

5. Pull up gathers; wrap this ruffle around rose and tack to secure.

Gathered Center Leaf

1. Cut a 7" length from 1"-wide green velvet ribbon. Fold ribbon in half.

2. Fold up one corner from ribbon, forming a point at tips of diagonal folds; pin fold in place.

3. Run a hand-gathering stitch from tip of diagonal fold.

4. Draw up gathers and open leaf. *Note: The gathers will be down center.* Knot thread to secure.

Hand-dyed Double-sided Satin Rose

1. Cut thirteen 5" lengths from one ribbon and two 5" lengths from another ribbon.

2. Stitch each petal in the following manner: Roll top edge down twice, then fold ribbon over at each end, holding each end with a pin.

3. Run a hand-gathering stitch along the bottom edge.

4. Pull to gather. Knot to secure.

5. To hand-dye petals: Mix a small amount of each dye color according to the manufacturer's instructions.

6. Place individual petals on a plastic surface such as recyclable plastic plates. Mist each petal lightly with water. Using cotton swab, touch each petal with plum dye in center and pink dye along outer edges. Lightly mist again, causing dye to spread. See photo on page 20. Allow to dry.

7. To assemble rose: Roll one petal. Stitch along bottom

to use for rose center.
Assemble rose by tacking
each petal in place with small
stitches as you move around
the rose.

Multipetal Flower Section

1. Divide ribbon into desired
   section lengths with a fabric
   marker, beginning and ending
   ⅛" from raw ends.

2. Run a hand-gathering stitch
   in a semicircular shape within
   each interval. Pull up gathers
   and secure thread.

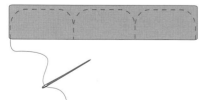

Ribbon Cocarde

1. Find center point
   of ribbon and fold
   down ends diago-
   nally so that bot-
   tom edges are even.

2. Fold each bottom end
   segment in half to-
   ward center and use
   a straight pin to hold
   this position. Repeat with
   each length.

3. Lay nine ribbon sections side
   by side. Run a hand-gathering
   stitch ⅓" from bottom fold.

4. Bring thread ends together
   and pull up gathers, creating a
   circle. Arrange each ribbon
   section; knot threads.

Rosette

1. Stitch short edges of ribbon length together.

2. Run a hand-gathering stitch near top edge of ribbon loop. Turn right side out.

3. Pull up gathers tightly; knot to secure.

Single-petal Flower Section

1. Run a hand-gathering stitch ⅛" from one raw edge of ribbon. Stitch down short side and continue stitching around corner, keeping stitches close to long edge.

2. Go around second corner and back up to top edge. Pull up gathers and secure thread by taking several small stitches.

Sweetheart Rose

1. Cut four 3" lengths from 1½"-wide silk ribbon (two ribbon widths). Cut 1½"-diameter circle from crinoline for center.

2. Tie a knot in center of one 3" length and stitch one end to each side of crinoline disk; arrange knot slightly off center.

3. Fold/roll bottom edge up twice, using approximately one-third of ribbon width. Pin down ends to hold roll and mist lightly with water; allow to dry.

4. Stitch as for a single-petal section, making certain to catch rolled-up edge on each end.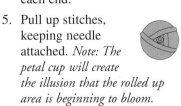

5. Pull up stitches, keeping needle attached. *Note: The petal cup will create the illusion that the rolled up area is beginning to bloom.*

6. Fit this cupped-petal section around crinoline disk, then bring ends to back and stitch in place.

7. Repeat for the next two petals, overlapping each to fit around knotted center.

Vintage Rose

1. Tie a knot in one end of wire-edged ribbon.

2. Find one end of wire in ribbon. Gently pull on wire, gathering ribbon as much as possible.

3. Wrap excess wire around other end of ribbon, cinching the ribbon.

4. Holding knotted end in one hand, begin to wrap gathered ribbon around several times, just below the knot.

5. When reaching the end of gathers (the cinched end) wrap excess wire around end; trim off any excess wire.

Note: Give the rose a vintage effect by rolling it into a ball and smashing it up. By flattening the rose with your hand, the bent wires will create a lovely vintage look. You can even wet it and toss it in the dryer.

VINTAGE ROSE BOOKMARK

MATERIALS TO GATHER

- Ribbons:
    - 1"-wide lavender wire-edged ribbon (¾ yd)
    - 1½"-wide green paisley ribbon (14")
    - 1½"-wide green pleated ribbon for background rosette (8")
- Felt scrap for back of rose
- Milliner's needle and hand-quilting thread
- Pin-backed fastener
- Velvet leaves (2)

INSTRUCTIONS

Note: The Vintage Rose is pinned onto the ribbon so that it can be removed and used as an accessory as well as a bookmark.

1. With 14" length of green paisely ribbon, turn the top edge down twice and hem.

2. Cut ribbon end at a diagonal.

3. Make a rosette from 8" pleated ribbon. Refer to Rosette on page 21.

4. Make a vintage rose from 1"-wide lavender wire-edged ribbon. Refer to Vintage Rose on page 22.

5. Center vintage rose over pleated rosette; hand-stitch or glue in place. Stitch or glue leaves onto back of rose.

6. Cut a small felt circle just large enough to cover back of rose. Stitch in place. Tack a pin-backed fastener to felt and pin to bookmark.

BUTTERFLY BOOKMARK

MATERIALS TO GATHER

- Ribbons:
    1"-wide green satin ribbon (⅓ yd)
    1¼"-wide green velvet ribbon (9")
    1½"-wide green satin ribbon (⅓ yd)
- Beading floss
- Beading needle
- Beads (2)
- Milliner's needle and hand-quilting thread
- Velvet leaves (2)
- Vintage pin

INSTRUCTIONS

1. Create rosette by cutting 9" ribbon length from 1¼"-wide velvet ribbon. Refer to Rosette on page 21.

2. Center 1" ribbon over 1½" ribbon and hand-stitch down center through both ribbons. Turn top edge down ½" twice and hem.

3. Fold bottom edge in half at center point with right sides together for "V" shape. Hand-stitch raw edges together ¼" from edge. Turn right side out. Finger-press.

4. Hand-stitch two beads onto bottom of bookmark.

5. Hand-stitch leaves onto back of flower.

6. Cut a small felt circle just large enough to cover back of flower. Stitch in place.

7. Pin vintage jewelry with rose onto bookmark.

LEAF BOOKMARK

MATERIALS TO GATHER

- Ribbons:
    - 1"-wide green satin ribbon (⅓ yd)
    - 1½"-wide green double-sided satin ribbon (⅓ yd)
- Hand-sewing needle and hand-sewing thread
- Tacky glue
- Velvet leaves (7)

INSTRUCTIONS

1. Center 1"-wide ribbon over 1½"-wide ribbon. Hand-stitch down center through both ribbons. Turn top edge down ⅛" twice and hem.

2. Fold bottom edge in half at center point with right sides together for "V" shape. Hand-stitch raw edges together ¼" from edge. Turn right side out. Finger-press.

3. Hand-stitch silk leaves down center of ribbons, slightly overlapping each leaf to hide the small stitches.

4. Lay velvet leaves slightly overlapping each other down center of bookmark and glue in place with a small amount of tacky glue. Allow to dry.

SOAP SACHET

- Ribbons:
    ⅛"-wide ivory ribbon to tie ends (¾ yd)
    ¾"-wide wire-edged ribbon (1 yd)
- Milliner's needle and hand-quilting thread
- Scented soap
- Sheer or wired silk fabric (12" x 8")
- Silk velvet leaves (3)

INSTRUCTIONS

1. Roll the bar of soap in center of fabric, overlapping fabric ends.

2. Cut narrow ribbon in half. Tie each end of fabric (like outside ends of a piece of hard candy) with the narrow ribbon.

3. Make three vintage roses from 12" of wire-edged ribbon. Refer to Vintage Rose on page 22.

4. Center roses and leaves onto soap. Using straight pins, attach to soap.

Note: I have fond memories of my Grandmother Tidwell sending my sisters and me scented soaps that she decorated for us. This sweet project reminds me of her lovely thoughtful gifts to us.

SWEETHEART OUTFIT

MATERIALS TO GATHER

- Ribbons:
    - 1"-wide pink silk ribbon (⅔ yd)
    - 1½"-wide green ruffled ribbon (1 yd)
    - 1½"-wide green satin ribbon (12")
    - 7mm light blue silk ribbon (⅓ yd)
    - 7mm light pink silk ribbon (3 yds)
- 2" sq. buckram
- Needles: 18 or 20 size chenille, milliner's and hand-quilting thread
- Pillowcase with a decorative edge (cut length depending on size)
- Size 1 child's T-shirt (can use sizes 6 months–6 years)
- Spray bottle with water
- Washable or disappearing-ink fabric marker

INSTRUCTIONS

1. Measure T-shirt approximately 2¾" below underarm and mark with fabric marker or straight pin. Cut straight across T-shirt from side to side. Set bottom section of T-shirt aside for hat.

2. Hand- or machine-stitch green ruffled ribbon around the neck of T-shirt.

3. Measure pillowcase for desired skirt length and add ¾". *Note: Pillowcase can be used for sizes 6 months–6 years.* Mark and cut.

4. Around top edge of pillow-case, run two rows of hand- or machine-gathering stitches to hold in place.

5. Mark center front and back of T-shirt and pillowcase, as well as sides with a straight pin or fabric marker; pin T-shirt and pillowcase right sides together along cut edge. Pull up gathers on pillowcase to fit. Stitch T-shirt to gath-ered pillowcase with a small zigzag or stretch stitch. Trim seam.

6. To make the little hat: First, turn T-shirt bottom inside out. On tube of fabric, sew side seam (to make hat nar-rower to fit child's head); trim off excess. Fold up bottom edge ¾" twice; tack every few inches. Run a gathering-stitch around cut end; pull up gathers tightly. Knot gath-ers to secure. Turn hat right side out.

7. Make two sweetheart roses from pink silk ribbon. Refer to Sweetheart Rose on page 21.

8. Make four folded leaves from green satin ribbon. Refer to Folded Leaves and Buds on page 18. Stitch one leaf onto both sides of roses.

9. For both roses, make three ¾" loops of 7mm light blue silk ribbon. Tack onto one side of each rose. Set one rose aside.

10. Fold 3 yds of 7mm light pink ribbon in half. Center and tie 4" double bow. Place double bow below the rose and leaves. Hand-stitch in place on neck center of dress.

11. Stitch remaining rose to hat. Make four 1½" loops from green ruffled trim. Place below rose and leaves; hand-stitch in place as shown below.

Step 11

Garden Sweater

MATERIALS TO GATHER

- Ribbons:
    - ¾"-wide cross-dyed green ribbon (1 yd)
    - 13mm dark rose-colored silk ribbon (1 yd)
    - 13mm light rose-colored silk ribbon (3 yds)
- 1"-wide decorative lace (⅔ yd)
- Beading floss
- Crinoline (1" circle)
- Different shades of green: threads, yarns and/or fibers (3 yds)
- Embroidery floss: gold, green, pink, sage green, variegated green
- Light pink metallic thread
- Needles: beading, milliner's, size 16 chenille and hand-quilting thread
- Small rose-colored buttons
- Small rose-colored heart crystal beads
- Spray bottle with water
- Sweater
- Washable or disappearing-ink fabric marker

INSTRUCTIONS

1. Using Leaf Pattern on page 39, cut approximately twenty leaves from lace. Set aside.

2. Using fabric marker, draw a vine that winds around neckline and sleeves of sweater.

3. Use a running stitch with six strands of sage green embroidery floss, embroider vine pattern. Refer to Running Stitch on page 14.

4. Using chenille needle with four or five strands of decorative embroidery floss as well as threads, yarns and/or fibers in shades of green, whipstitch the running stitch. Refer to Whipped Running Stitch on page 14.

5. Pin lace leaves along vine as shown below.

6. Hand-stitch around the leaves with light pink metallic thread.

7. Use ribbon stitch to make a few buds with the 13mm rose-colored silk ribbon. Refer to Ribbon Stitch on page 14.

8. Accent one side of each bud with a leaf-stitch of sheer or green ribbon (to resemble an emerging bud) as shown below. Refer to Leaf Stitch on page 14.

Step 5

Step 8

9. Along vine, randomly stitch rose-colored heart crystal beads, small French knots, beads, and rose-colored buttons as shown at right and below. Refer to French Knot on page 14.

10. Make a sweetheart rose from dark rose sheer silk ribbon. Refer to Sweetheart Rose on page 21.

Back view of Garden Sweater

11. To create leaves: Make three ribbon stitches with ¾"-wide cross-dyed sheer ribbon. Place around and just under rose. Stitch sweetheart rose to sweater. See Placement Diagram below for placement.

12. Decorate sleeve ends in the same manner with gold embroidery floss.

13. With gold embroidery floss, make a running stitch around neck edge.

Leaf Pattern
Actual Size

Placement Diagram

Knitted Ribbon Scarf

MATERIALS TO GATHER

- Ribbon:
    ¾"-wide pink hand-dyed silk ribbon for knitting
        (1 skein)
- Size 50 knitting needle

INSTRUCTIONS

1. Cut twenty 22" lengths of ribbon for fringe; set aside.

2. Cast on fourteen stitches onto knitting needle. Using garter stitch, knit until you have achieved the desired length for the scarf. *Note: This scarf is approximately 60" long. The number of rows knitted is determined by the tightness of stitches and the width of ribbon.* Bind off knitting.

3. Fold a piece of fringe in half. Loop folded edge through end of knitted scarf. Repeat. Space fringe pieces evenly across both scarf ends.

4. To create a diamond effect of knotted ribbon fringe: Bring two single strands of fringe together and tie knots 1" below scarf edge.

5. For the next row of knots, alternate with one strand from two separate knots and knot those together 1½" below last row. Bring the two original strands together and knot again 1½" below the last.

6. Trim excess fringe as desired.

Project 8

Embellished Camisole

MATERIALS TO GATHER
- Ribbons:
    - 13mm green silk ribbon for leaf ribbon stitches (¾ yd)
    - 13mm hand-dyed pink-ivory silk ribbon (9")
    - 13mm pink/peach silk ribbon for seven outer-rose ribbon stitches (1 yd)
- Beading floss
- Crystal beads
- Needles: beading, size 13 chenille and hand-quilting thread
- Silk camisole
- Washable or disappearing-ink fabric marker

INSTRUCTIONS

1. Make a cabbage rose with 9" of 13mm hand-dyed pink-ivory silk ribbon. Refer to Cabbage Rose on page 17. Set aside.

2. Using fabric marker, mark placement on silk of outer petals and leaves on both sides of petals.

3. Make three ribbon stitches on each side of rose for leaves. Stitch crystal beads around rose to resemble dewdrops.

4. Center and stitch onto top edge of camisole.

TAPESTRY PILLOW

MATERIALS TO GATHER

- Ribbons:
    ¾"-wide cross-dyed green sheer ribbon (1½ yds)
    1"-wide green silk ribbon (1 yd)
    1½"-wide green silk ribbon (15")
    1¾"-wide hand-dyed peach/yellow silk ribbon (4 yds)
    7mm green silk ribbon
- 11"-diameter embroidery hoop
- Beading floss
- Beads
- Cord trim (1 yd)
- Fiberfill stuffing
- Green embroidery floss
- Needles: beading, chenille 13, 22 or equivalent, embroidery
    and hand-quilting thread
- Old damask tablecloth or other background fabric
- Tapestry fabric (⅓ yd)
- Thin fleece batting (⅓ yd)
- Velvet leaves
- Vintage hat netting (1 yd)
- Washable or disappearing-ink fabric marker

1. Using 1¾" hand-dyed silk ribbon, make two large folded and rolled roses from 16" length. Refer to Folded and Rolled Roses on page 17.

2. Make one bud from 9" length, and three smaller buds from 6" lengths. Refer to Folded Leaves and Buds on page 18. Set aside.

3. Place background fabric in embroidery hoop. *Note: I used an old damask tablecloth over a layer of poly fleece to give it more body.* Draw simple guidelines for rose leaf placement with fabric marker.

4. Make one cabbage rose. Refer to Cabbage Rose on page 17.

5. With long stitches, make stems using 7mm green silk ribbon, slightly rolled. Couch in place with a few stitches of green floss where it curves.

6. Embroider ribbon and leaf-stitch ribbon leaves where indicated on guidelines or on

either side of a ribbon bud or small rose. Refer to Ribbon and Leaf Stitch on page 14.

7. Tack on a few velvet leaves and beads.

8. Turn project over and hand-tack loose ends from large ribbon leaves.

9. To make pillow: Cut one 12" tapestry circle for pillow back and two 5" x 36" lengths from tapestry fabric for sides.

10. Place the two 5" x 36" pieces with right sides together. Stitch 5" sides together, using ½" seam allowance. Press seam open.

11. Run two rows of gathering stitches on each side of the 35" lengths of the fabric; pull up gathers tightly.

12. Lay with right sides together around background material (pillow top); pin gathers evenly. Stitch in place.

13. Repeat for pillow bottom, leaving an area open large enough to turn pillow right side out.

14. Trim seams, clip curves, and carefully turn right side out.

15. Stuff with fiberfill.

16. Hand-stitch cord around pillow edge.

17. Tack the vintage hat netting around pillow as shown below.

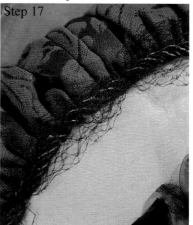
Step 17

SALT SHAKER TASSEL

- Ribbons:
    - ⅛"-wide gold ribbon (10")
    - 1"-wide dark pink velvet ribbon for rosette tassels (15")
    - 1½"-wide fuchsia velvet ribbon for rosette tassels (18")
- Assorted materials: embroidery flosses, fibers,
    ribbons, trims, yarns (approximately 5')
- Cardboard (5" x 10")
- Embroidery floss (12")
- Gold thread
- Industrial-strength glue
- Leaves (5)
- Salt shaker
- Size 20 chenille needle or any needle with large eye and
    hand-quilting thread
- Small figurine (optional)
- Trim (5')
- Wire (8")

INSTRUCTIONS

1. Fold cardboard in half lengthwise, creating 5" square. Start at open end of cardboard and wrap threads around cardboard from open end to folded end until you have covered cardboard with 7–10 layers of trim. *Note: How many times you wrap is directly proportional to amount of trims used and their thickness.*

2. Cut 12" length of embroidery floss (all six strands). Thread it through needle. Slide needle under wrapped fibers near fold in cardboard. Slide very sharp scissors between two layers of cardboard at open end. Cut through all loops of thread. With threads on top, carefully open cardboard. Lift ends of embroidery floss, pulling up threads to tie a knot around the fibers. Tie a very tight knot and knot again. Smooth the length of the tassel skirt and wrap with another length of embroidery floss ¾" down from center. To create a really full tassel: Flip tassel upside down and distribute fibers evenly around the center.

3. To create loop to hang tassel: Bend an 8" length of wire in half and push ends up through bottom of shaker and out pouring holes. Make a little wire loop and twist ends together. Trim off excess wire. Thread a 10" length of narrow ribbon through loop to hang finished salt shaker tassel. Tie a double knot and bow at the opposite end. Glue tassel to bottom of salt shaker.

4. Make two ribbon rosettes, one from 1"-wide velvet ribbon and one from 1½"-wide velvet ribbon. Refer to Rosette on page 21.

5. Lay smaller rosette over larger one, right sides facing up; glue or stitch together. Under bottom edge of larger rosette, glue leaves. On bottom of salt shaker, glue rosettes. Under rosettes, glue tassel. Allow to dry; trim tassel ends.

Alternative Idea:

To make the Teapot Tassel shown above, follow Steps 1–3 on page 50. Tie a 1" teardrop with strong gold thread and suspend it slightly below tassel bottom. Glue threads inside the tassel to hold the crystal in place.

51

CHRISTMAS STOCKING

MATERIALS TO GATHER

- Ribbons:
    - 1½"-wide silver mesh ribbon (¾ yd)
    - 2¾"-wide taupe ribbon (¾ yd)
- 1½"-wide sage green fringe (¾ yd)
- Beading floss
- Cord trim (8")
- Needles: beading, milliner's and hand-quilting thread
- Sage green Christmas stocking
- Vintage buttons
- Vintage crystal beads
- Vintage flowers
- Vintage sequined leaves

Tip: This is a great way to show-case a beloved piece of vintage jewelry. Simply pin it onto the top of stocking.

INSTRUCTIONS

1. With taupe ribbon, measure around top of stocking and add ½"; Cut. Fold in half, right sides together, making a loop. Stitch short ends together and turn right side

out. Place around top of stocking and hand-tack in place. Repeat with silver mesh ribbon. Place over taupe ribbon; stitch in place.

2. Hand-stitch appropriate length of fringe to stocking just under bottom edge of taupe trim.

3. Tack vintage sequined leaves, flowers, and buttons as shown below with hand-quilting thread or beading floss. Stitch beads with beading floss around stocking at approximately 1½" intervals.

4. For hanger: Securely hand-stitch 8" length of cord to inside edge of one side of stocking, with folded edge extending 2" above stocking.

5. Add other buttons or trims as desired.

Step 3

CRYSTAL ORNAMENT

- Ribbons:
  1"-wide blue ribbon for two rosettes (10")
  1½"-wide green silk ribbon for bow (22")
- 22-gauge wire or equivalent
- Circular piece of vintage crystal costume jewelry
- Industrial-strength glue
- Milliner's needle and hand-quilting thread
- Piece of fishing line to hang ornament
- Silk leaves

1. Thread a piece of wire through hole in top of crystal. Make a loop; twist the ends together.

2. Make two rosettes from 1"-wide ribbon. Refer to Rosette on page 21.

3. Arrange silk leaves slightly behind the top rosette; tack in place.

4. Make 3" bow from silk ribbon.

5. Lay one rosette over the other, right sides facing up; glue or stitch together.

6. Pin jewelry in center of rosette. Sandwich wire between two rosettes; stitch or glue together.

7. Suspend from a piece of fishing line tied to wire.

Alternative Idea

To make the Crystal Ornament above follow Step 1 of Crystal Ornament on page 55, then make one rosette from 1"-wide ribbon. Refer to Rosette on page 21. Pin jewelry in center of rosette. Suspend from a piece of fishing line tied to wire.

SCRAPBOOK POSY

- Ribbons:
    ⅜"-wide light green velvet ribbon (½ yd)
    1"-wide cross-dyed blue organdy ribbon (1½ yds)
    1"-wide light green velvet ribbon (25")
    1½"-wide blue sheer organdy ribbon (25")
- Circular piece of vintage crystal costume jewelry
- Double-sided tape
- Industrial-strength glue
- Milliner's needle and hand-quilting thread
- Ruler
- Scrapbook (6½" x 8")
- Velvet leaves (2)

INSTRUCTIONS

1. With ruler, very lightly pencil a guideline ½" from top of album. Mark guideline from inside front of album jacket to inside back. Apply double-sided tape along this mark.

2. Press ⅜"-wide light green velvet ribbon onto double-sided tape. Divide 1"-wide ribbon in half and thread through opening on side of book.

3. Make two rosettes, one with sheer ribbon and one with velvet ribbon. Refer to Rosette on page 21.

4. Arrange velvet leaves slightly behind top rosette and tack in place.

5. Pin jewelry to center of rosette. Glue to front of scrapbook.

COCARDE SNOWFLAKE

MATERIALS TO GATHER

- Ribbons:
    1½"-wide silver-mesh ribbon (12")
    1½"-wide silver wire-mesh ribbon (7½")
    1½"-wide silver wire-mesh ribbon (45")
- 1⅛" rhinestone button
- Milliner's needle and hand-quilting thread
- Wire or ribbon to hang finished ornament (10")

INSTRUCTIONS

1. Cut nine 5" pieces from 45" length wire-mesh ribbon to make ribbon cocarde ornament. See Ribbon Cocarde Ornament on page 17.

2. Make two rosettes; one from 7½" wire-mesh ribbon and the other from 12" silver-mesh ribbon. Refer to Rosette on page 21.

3. To decorate both sides of snowflake: Stitch wire-mesh rosette with a button to center on one side, and silver-mesh rosette on the other.

4. Use a piece of wire or ribbon to hang.

Alternative Idea

To make Snowflake Ornament shown above, follow Step 1–2 of Cocarde Ornament on page 17. Stitch wire-mesh rosette with 1¾" silver craft medallion to one side, and remaining silver mesh rosette on the other side.

Alternative Idea

To make Cocarde Decorative Handbag shown above, follow Step 1 of Cocarde Ornament on page 60, using eleven 4" lengths of ¾"-wide silver ribbon. Turn over cocarde, making the back the front. Stitch a silver craft medallion to center of cocarde. Tack to front of handbag.

63

NEEDLE HOLDER

- Ribbons:
  - ¾"-wide green silk ribbon (9")
  - 1"-wide purple-green silk ribbon (14")
  - 4mm light green ribbon for ribbon stitches (1 yd)
- ½"-wide gold-metallic lace (4")
- Austrian crystal beads (3)
- Beaded chain (30")
- Green wool felt (8" x 11")
- Needles: beading, size 22 chenille needle
- Photocopier
- Threads: beading, gold embroidery

1. Enlarge Heart Pattern and Pocket Pattern on page 66 200% on photocopier. Cut two heart pieces and one pocket piece from green felt.

2. Hand-stitch gold lace to left side of pocket. Stitch a gold running stitch along top-right pocket edge.

3. Lay pocket over heart front; tack four corners in place.

4. Alternate stitching gold French knots with light green ribbon stitches around heart. Refer to French Knot on page 14. *Note: This will secure bottom of pocket to heart bottom.*

5. Stitch three crystal beads to the top heart as shown in photo on opposite page.

6. Leaf-stitch two ribbon leaves from 4½" of ¾"-wide silk ribbon. Refer to Leaf Stitch on page 14.

7. Make a folded and rolled rose from 1"-wide purple-green ribbon. Refer to Folded and Rolled Rose on page 18.

8. Stitch rose and leaves to pocket. *Note: Be careful not to stitch through the pocket.*

9. Attach one end of chain to each side of heart with small stitches. *Note: Mine was from an old broken necklace.*

10. Stitch second heart piece, over back of decorated heart, with small invisible stitches around edges.

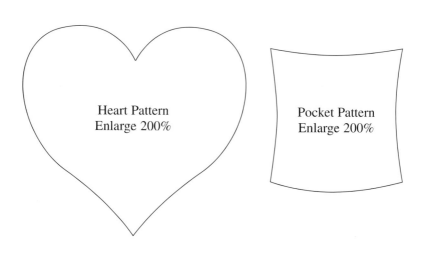

Heart Pattern
Enlarge 200%

Pocket Pattern
Enlarge 200%

PANSY HAIR BARRETTE

MATERIALS TO GATHER

- Ribbons:
    - ¼"-wide purple ombre ribbon (5")
    - 1½"-wide deep purple velvet ribbon (9")
- 1"-wide white lace (9")
- 1½"-wide gold trim (9")
- 3" hair barrette
- Beading floss
- Felt oval (2" x 1")
- Green multifaceted beads (12)
- Needles: beading, milliner's and hand-quilting thread
- Rhinestone sprays
- Small rose-colored bead for center beading (1)
- Velvet leaves (2)
- Washable or disappearing-ink fabric marker

INSTRUCTIONS

1. Make two single-petal sections each from 4" length of deep purple velvet. Refer to Single-petal Flower Section on page 21.

2. For bottom outer petals, lay lace and gold trim with one long edge aligned and make a single-petal section, using these two trims as one.

3. Mark inner petal flower section at 2½", 2½", and 4".

4. Make a multipetal section using measurements from Step 2. Refer to Multipetal Flower Section on page 20.

5. Pull up the gathers and bring the raw edges together, tuck them to the back side and stitch. *Note: This will give you a lovely pansy with two smaller sections at the top.*

6. Assemble flower by overlapping the single-petal sections by ¾"; stitch together. Lay top petals with the three-petal section and lace/gold trim section below. Stitch together.

7. Make 1" bow from ¼"-wide ombre ribbon.

8. Tack a small round bead to center of bow. Stitch to center of pansy.

9. Use three 4" sections to make decorative beaded accents by wiring one long faceted bead to each section. Twist ends together individually and as a group.

10. Add a few rhinestone sprays by hand-stitching over the wires to hold them in place behind the barrette.

11. Tack two silk leaves to side of pansy.

12. Add a few stitched beads to leaves, if desired.

13. Turn flower over; stitch a small felt oval to back.

14. Tack each end of floral piece onto a barrette.

Note: The barrette used in this project was found in the bridal section of a craft store.

PANSY RIBBON FRAME

MATERIALS TO GATHER

- Ribbons:
  - ⅜"-wide green striped ribbon (40")
  - ¾"-wide green velvet ribbon (24")
  - 1"-wide deep purple velvet ribbon for two 5½" single-petal sections (11")
  - 1"-wide green velvet ribbon (7")
  - 1½"-wide fuchsia velvet ribbon (5")
  - 1½"-wide pink sheer organdy ribbon for two 5½" single-petal sections (11")
- ¾"-wide gold trim (5")
- Felt oval (1" x 2")
- Frame
- Green vintage jewelry
- Milliner's needle and hand-quilting thread
- Pin-backed fastener
- Tacky glue

INSTRUCTIONS

1. Make two single-petal sections from sheer ribbon and deep purple ribbon. Refer to Single-petal Flower Section on page 21. Make one single-petal flower section from the fuchsia ribbon.

2. Make one gathered center leaf from 1"-wide green velvet ribbon. Refer to Gathered Center Leaf on page 19.

3. Cut 24" green velvet ribbon into three 8" sections. Knot each length in the center. Lay them side by side. "Fan them out" by tacking bottom edges together.

4. Assemble flower by overlapping the sheer petals by ¾" and stitch together; repeat for the deep velvet. Stitch the two outer-petal sections together. Roll ¾"-wide gold trim tightly; tack outer edge down. *Note: This makes a great flower center.*

5. Lay trim inside gathered edge of bottom petal.

6. Stitch flower together with tiny tack stitches.

7. Stitch on gathered center leaf and knotted ribbon.

8. Pin on vintage jewelry.

9. Turn flower over. Cut a piece of felt to stitch to back of flower for support. Stitch a pin-backed fastener onto felt.

10. Glue ⅜"-wide green striped ribbon around outer edge of frame.

11. Cut, then glue a small circle of felt to top of frame to pin flower in place (and optionally remove later).

Heirloom Rose Hat

MATERIALS TO GATHER

- Ribbons:
  - 1"-wide rose-colored pleated ribbon (9")
  - 1"-wide rose-colored satin ribbon for three-petal section (11")
  - 1¼"-wide rose-colored fringed ribbon for three-petal section (22")
  - 1¼"-wide rose-colored tapestry ribbon for three-petal section (11")
  - 1½"-wide rose-colored wire-edged ribbon for two-petal section (7")
- 2"-diameter cardboard circle
- 2"-wide lace (12")
- 3"-diameter fabric circle
- 22-gauge wire (36")
- Beading floss
- Crystal beads
- Hat with lace trim
- Needles: beading, milliner's and hand-quilting thread
- One large crystal bead
- Pin-backed fastener
- Small seed beads (60)
- Vintage gold/rhinestone leaf-shaped brooch
- Vintage green leaves (5)
- Vintage rhinestone flower pin

1. To make a beaded flower center: Cut six 6" lengths from wire; bend lengths in half to find center.

2. Slide fifteen beads onto a piece of wire and twist ends to make a beaded loop in center, repeat with four wires.

3. Slide large crystal bead to center of last wire and twist wire under bead. Arrange smaller bead loops around large bead and twist all wires together.

4. Make two sets of three-petal sections, one from rose-colored satin ribbon and one from and tapestry ribbon. Refer to Multipetal Flower Section on page 20.

5. Make two-petal section from wire-edged ribbon.

6. Arrange three petal sections and two petal sections around this flower center, tacking each one in place as you go. Finish by adding lace and pleated ribbon.

7. Run a hand-gathering stitch around fabric circle and pull up gathers slightly. Place over 2" cardboard circle and pull up gathers; tightly knot to secure. *Note: This makes a nice backing to glue to the back of a rose. Add a pin-backed fastener to this circle and just pin it to the hat or desired item.*

8. Pin or stitch leaves and jewelry in place.

9. Hand-stitch beads on roses to resemble dewdrops.

10. Hand-stitch leaves under rose. Pin rose to hat.

11. Attach brooch and flower pin to center front of hat.

Note: This is called the Heirloom Rose Hat because it was created with lots of small bits of treasured heirloom ribbons and trims. Use a piece of your mother's wedding lace, a snippet of ribbon from your bouquet, or even a handmade doily found in the bottom of a hope chest. Treasure these heirlooms and give them a fresh new outlook.

BRIDAL ROSE BAG

MATERIALS TO GATHER

- Ribbon:
  ½"-wide sheer silver ribbon (22")
- Crystal beads
- Glass seed beads (1 hank)
- Ivory handbag
- Ivory silk fabric (⅛ yd)
- Light ivory wired silk fabric (⅛ yd)
- Vintage feather pendant

INSTRUCTIONS

1. Cut and tear both fabrics into 2"-wide strips. Make ribbons from 2" strips for a total of 33". Refer to Making Ribbons on page 12.

2. Make fabric bridal rose from ribbon strips. Refer to Fabric Bridal Rose on page 17.

3. Make three Folded Leaves from ribbon strips. Refer to Folded Leaves and Buds on page 18. Stitch leaves on either side of rose.

4. Tack a few crystals in center and around petals to resemble dewdrops.

5. Hand-stitch rose to front of handbag. Stitch entire hank of beads under rose.

6. Hand-rip silver ribbon along grain line, and tie into bow. Stitch below one side of ribbon on purse.

7. Pin on vintage feather pendant as shown in photo on opposite page.

RIBBON PLACE CARD

MATERIALS TO GATHER

- Ribbon:
    ⅜"-wide ivory ribbon (22")
- Gold embossed cardstock (4½" x 3¾")
- Handmade paper (3½" x 2½")
- Metallic gold pen
- Rhinestone button
- Size 18 chenille needle
- Tacky glue

INSTRUCTIONS

1. Fold embossed paper in half at center to create basic place card. Gently tear edges of handmade paper irregularly.

2. Using gold pen, write the guest's name on paper.

3. Glue the paper to front of place card.

4. Thread chenille needle with ivory ribbon. Make a stitch in and out of one corner and tie a bow.

5. Make loose straight stitches with one end on the bow streamer through the paper.

6. Thread needle on other streamer and make loose loops on that side as well.

7. Stitch a small rhinestone button over the bow center. *Note: This also helps to keep the bow tied.*

ROSE SACHET

- Ribbons:
    - 1"-wide cross-dyed organdy (22")
    - 1½"-wide double-sided lavender satin ribbon (2 yds)
    - 1½"-wide double-sided sage green satin ribbon (10")
    - 4½"-wide netting ribbon (11")
- 1½"-diameter felt circle
- 4½"-wide vintage lace (11")
- Cotton swab
- Dried lavender flowers (1 cup)
- Fabric dyes: pink, plum
- Milliner's needle and hand-quilting thread
- Pin backed fastener
- Silk leaves (3)
- Spray bottle with water

INSTRUCTIONS

1. Make a hand-dyed double-sided satin rose. Refer to Hand-dyed Double-sided Satin Rose on page 19.

2. Stitch leaves onto back of flower. Cut a small felt circle just large enough to cover back of flower. Stitch in place. Tack a pin-backed fastener to felt.

3. To make sachet bag: Stitch vintage lace over netting on all sides. Fold in half; hand-stitch 4½" sides to create a bag. Fill with dried lavender flowers. Tie with organdy ribbon; pin flower in center of ribbon.

SIMPLE GIFT BAG

- Ribbons:
    - 1"-wide green ribbon with sheer edge
    - 1"-wide green tapestry ribbon (7")
    - 1"-wide silver mesh ribbon for bow (22")
- Beads
- Fabric glue
- Gift bag
- Needles: milliner's and hand-quilting thread
- Rhinestone button
- Unfinished needlepoint

1. Cut leaf shapes from unfinished area of needlepoint.

2. Glue a few beads on leaves in unfinished areas.

3. Make two rosettes, one from tapestry ribbon and one from green ribbon with sheer edge. Refer to Rosette on page 21.

4. Place rosette with sheer edge on top of remaining rosette.

5. Glue on rhinestone button.

6. Tie a bow with silver mesh ribbon. Place bow under rosette. Tack rose onto gift bag with needlepoint leaves.

Tip: Unfinished needlepoint is inexpensive and easy to find at yard sales.

Fluted Rose

MATERIALS TO GATHER

- Ribbon:
  25mm ivory crepe georgette ribbon (59")
- Cream flower stamens (12)
- Milliner's needle and hand-quilting thread

INSTRUCTIONS

1. Cut 59" length from 25mm ivory crepe georgette ribbon. To create up and down folds (flute): Begin with a running stitch along bottom edge of one end of ribbon. See Fluting Diagram below.

Fluting Diagram

2. Fold ribbon up and down, and make 1¾" loops placing finished ribbon edge on one loop in center of next loop, in an overlapping zigzag fashion. Pin in place along bottom edge as you create folds along length of ribbon.

3. Use a running stitch ¼" from bottom folded edge of overlapping loops, connecting them together. Pull up thread to slightly gather. Tie off thread.

4. To make rose: Loosely roll gathered edge. Tack with a few stitches to secure. For center: Fold twelve stamens in half. Tie stamens in center with wire. Tuck into center of rose. Tack to secure.

TWISTED ROSE ACCENT

MATERIALS TO GATHER

- Ribbons:
    - ¾"-wide gold velvet ribbon for large rose (22")
    - ¾"-wide gold velvet ribbon for small rose (14")
    - 1½"-wide green silk ribbon for folded leaves
- 1" circle crinoline (2)
- 3" sq. green felt
- Gift bag
- Small and large hat or corsage pins (2)
- Industrial-strength glue
- Milliner's needle and hand-quilting thread
- Old piece of light green hat netting
- Pin-backed fastener

INSTRUCTIONS

1. To make a twisted rose: Pinch one end of 22" length of ribbon in half and tack it down to center of circle of crinoline. *Note: Crinoline circle should be slightly smaller than the size of desired finished rose.*

2. Pin a large hat or corsage pin to center of circle, holding the circle with the ribbon extend-

ing with left hand. Twist the ribbon with right hand to resemble a rope.

3. Gently wind twisted ribbon around center and under each extending end of pin. Spiraling the ribbon outward and away from center.

4. Tack the ribbons to crinoline and remove pin.

5. Repeat with remaining length of ribbon.

6. Make one to three folded leaves. Refer to Folded Leaves and Buds on page 18.

7. Stitch leaves onto either side of twisted roses.

8. Glue felt square onto back of rose grouping. Stitch pin-backed fastener to back of felt. *Note: By gluing felt square onto twisted rose grouping and stitching a pin-backed fastener onto the back of the felt, the twisted Roses can be removed and used as a brooch or clothing item accessory.*

9. Tie netting onto gift bag. Pin grouping onto netting.

Alternative Idea

To make the Twisted Accent Rose Pins shown above, follow Steps 1–8 of Twisted Rose Accent on pages 86–88.

FRINGED SWEATER

- Ribbon:
    1½"-wide peach sheer organdy ribbon (7 yds)
- Needles: hand-sewing; large tapestry needle size 16 or 18
    and hand-sewing thread
- Peach wired silk fabric (1½ yds)

INSTRUCTIONS

1. Tear fabric and ribbon into long 1½"-wide strips.

2. Thread one end of a strip into tapestry needle. Bring needle up from inside of sweater along one side. Run long gathering stitches about 2"–3" long across sweater front as shown at right and on opposite page. Randomly tie small bows with ribbon ends.

3. Make 3–4 rows across front of sweater.

Step 2

4. Using hand-sewing needle and thread, secure strips on underside of sweater by tacking strips in place.

5. For sleeves: Alternate 1" long stitches with ribbon and fabric strips. Tie knots, leaving ends 1½" long. Trim ends on a diagonal.

6. Repeat Step 5 around each sleeve, covering bottom 2" of each sleeve end.

Note: This Mermaid Tassel is a variation of the Salt Shaker Tassel on page 48.

Katheryn Tidwell Bieber has been designing and creating since she was three years old. Among her first designs was a pair of knee-high boots made entirely of mud (her mother was less than thrilled). Since then, she has moved on to designing for *Butterick, Vogue, Simplicity, McCalls, Family Circle,* and *Woman's Day* magazines, and more. Katheryn has been the cohost and designer on Aleene's Creative Living, Our Place, Home Matters, and many other television shows. She has taught classes and workshops all over the country and is currently speaking on "from Survival to Celebration: Keys to creating a joyful life." She resides in Santa Barbara, California, with her husband and five children.

Katheryn finds the easiest way for her to create beautiful things is to fill her heart with beauty, bliss, and joy; then let that creative energy flow through her.

CONVERSION CHART

inches to millimeters and centimeters
(mm-millimeters, cm-centimeters)

inches	mm	cm	inches	cm	inches	cm
⅛	3	0.3	11	27.9	31	78.7
¼	6	0.6	12	30.5	32	81.3
⅜	10	1.0	13	33.0	33	83.8
½	13	1.3	14	35.6	34	86.4
⅝	16	1.6	15	38.1	35	88.9
¾	19	1.9	16	40.6	36	91.4
⅞	22	2.2	17	43.2	37	94.0
1	25	2.5	18	45.7	38	96.5
1¼	32	3.2	19	48.3	39	99.1
1½	38	3.8	20	50.8	40	101.6
1¾	44	4.4	21	53.3	41	104.1
2	51	5.1	22	55.9	42	106.7
3	76	7.6	23	58.4	43	109.2
4	102	10.2	24	61.0	44	111.8
5	127	12.7	25	63.5	45	114.3
6	152	15.2	26	66.0	46	116.8
7	178	17.8	27	68.6	47	119.4
8	203	20.3	28	71.1	48	121.9
9	229	22.9	29	73.7	49	124.5
10	254	25.4	30	76.2	50	127.0

INDEX